Push and

David and Penny Glover

OXFORD

UNIVERSITY PRESS

Push the swing.

push

Pull the string.

pull

Dad pushes the buggy.

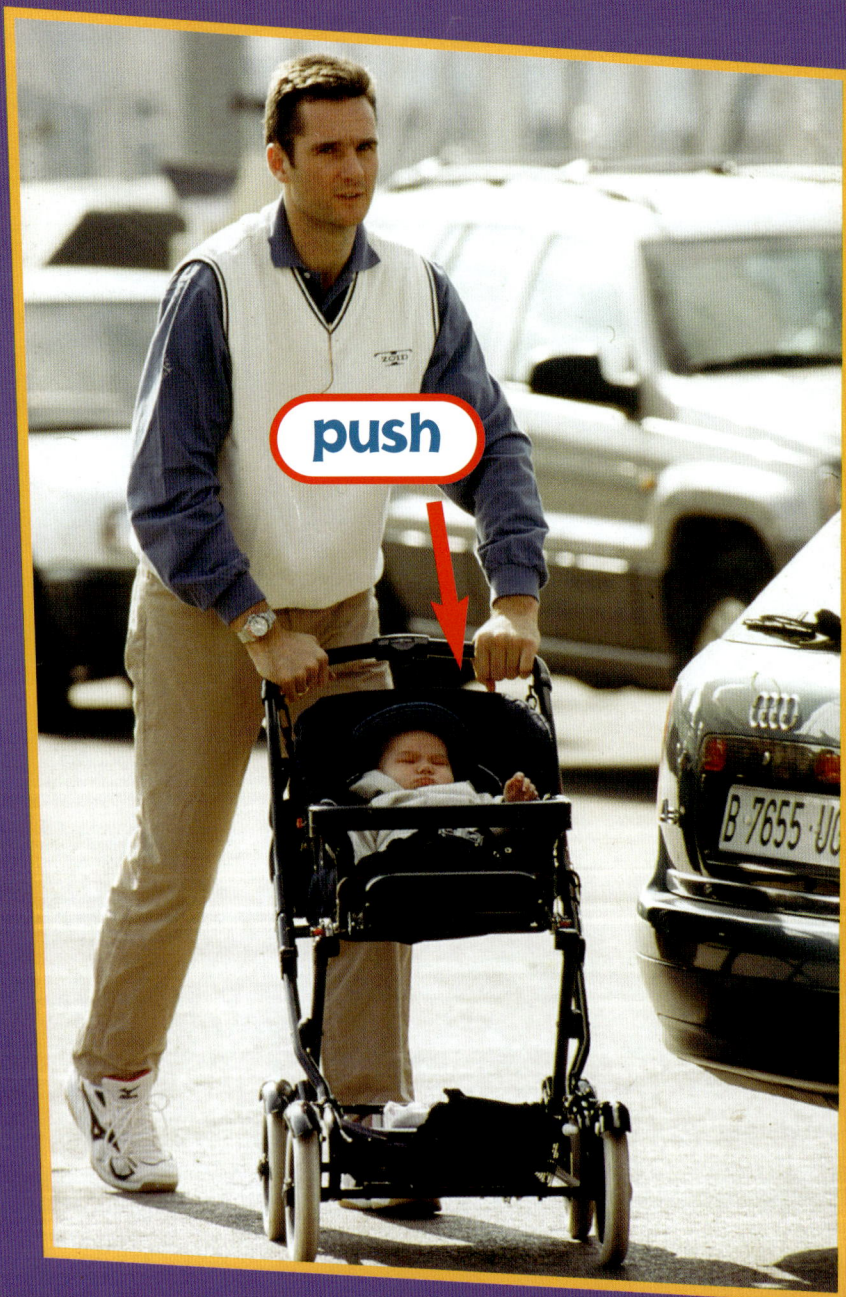

push

My dog pulls me.

pull

Mum pushes the trolley.

push

trolley

Dad pulls the case.

pull

case

My sister pushes the barrow.

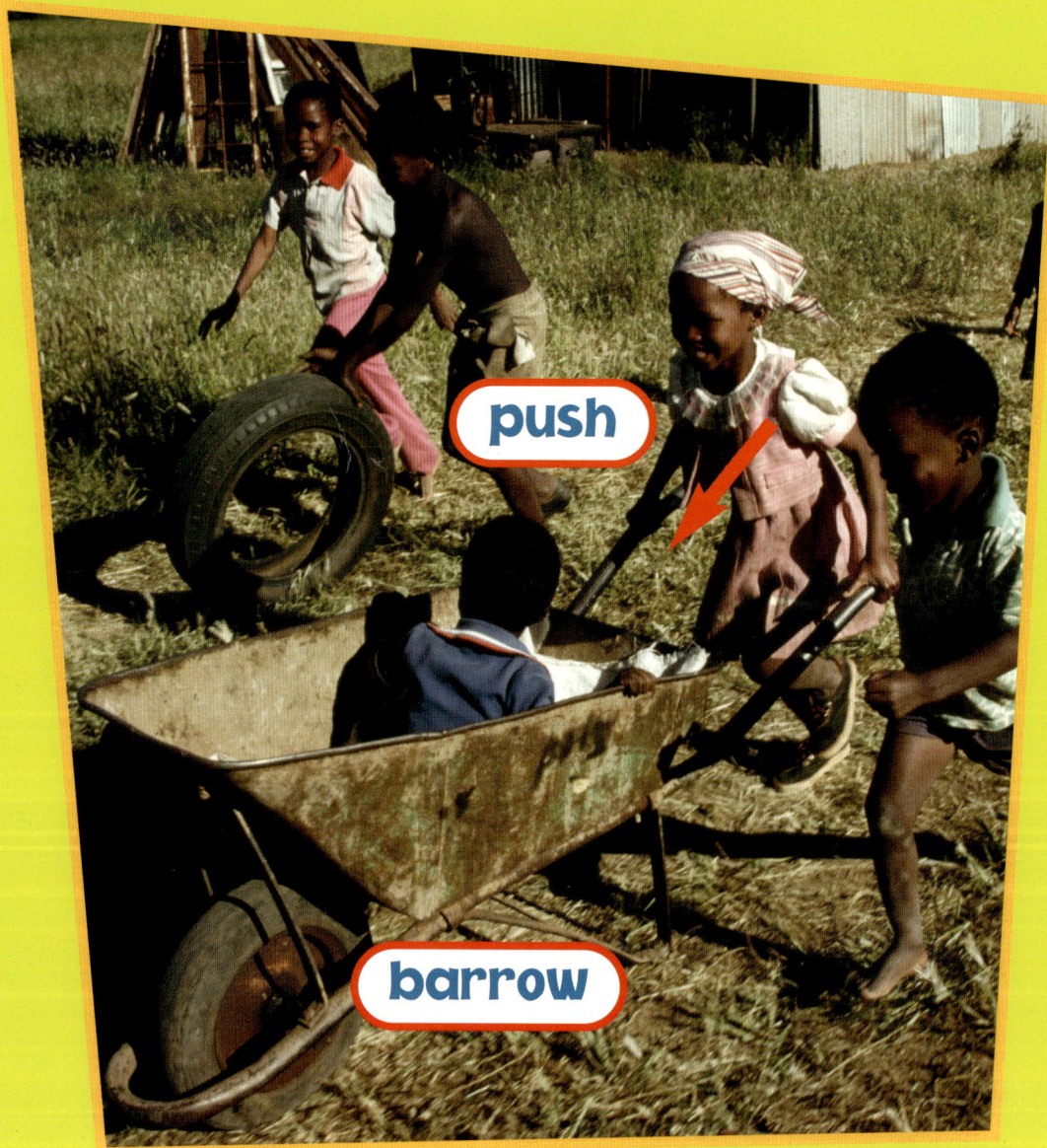

push

barrow

I pull up some weeds.

pull

My sister pulls the sledge.

pull

sledge

We all push the snowball.

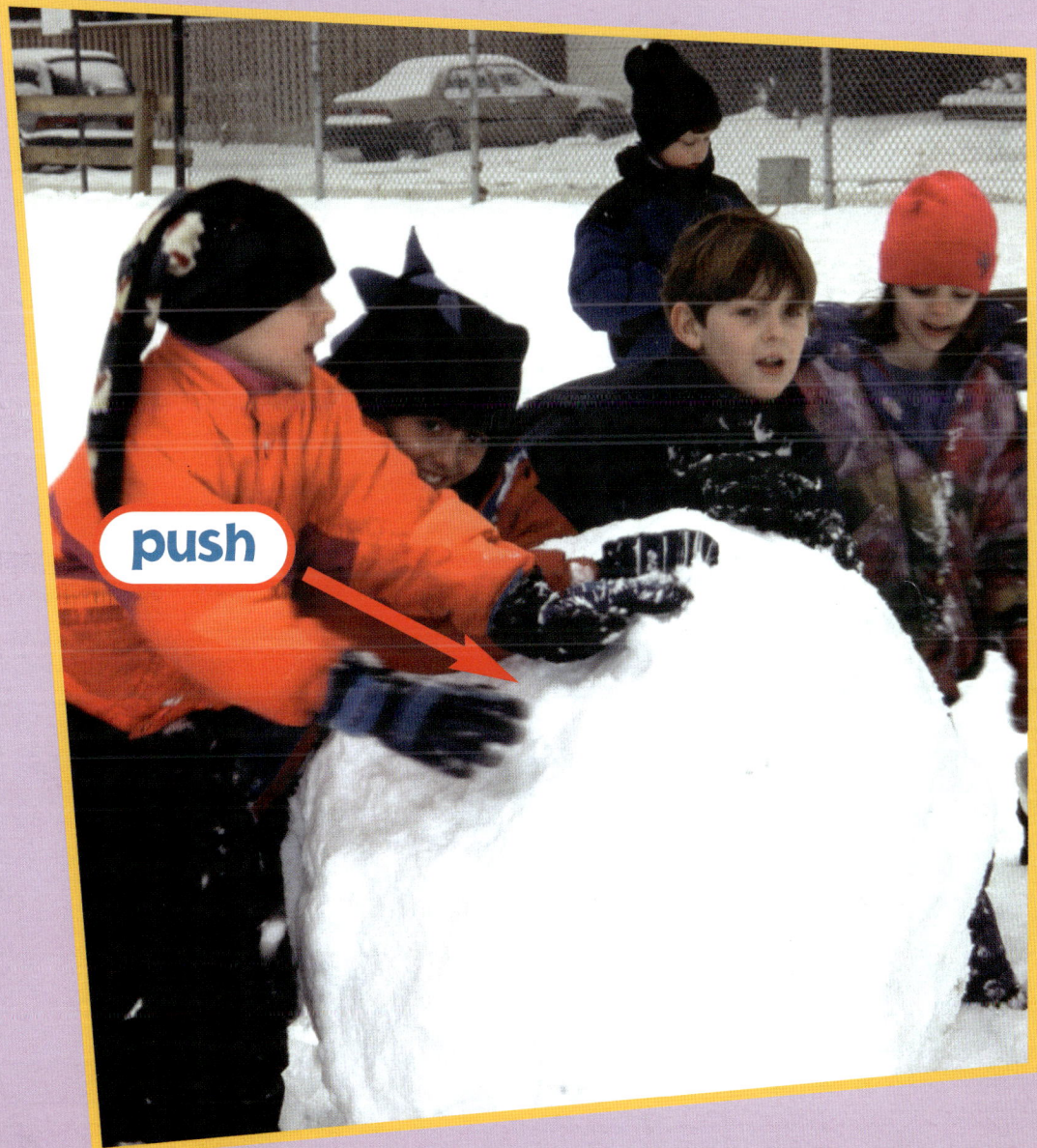

push

11

The car pulls the caravan.

caravan

pull

The farmer pushes the gate.

push

farmer

13

The children push the roundabout.

roundabout

push

We all pull the rope.

pull

pull

Pushes and pulls make things go.

push

pull

push

pull

push

pull